KEEPING HOPE ALIVE

Who finds refuge in Britain?

This book about refugees in Britain is an initiative of **Jesuit Refugee Service** in Britain. JRS hopes that it will enable people to be better informed, and so better able to think out how they can respond as Christians to the needs of refugees and people who are in the process of applying for asylum. JRS hopes that those who have read this book will share their insights with others.

Thanks to all those who met to reflect on this material including: Maria Elena Arana, Michael Barnes, Bernard Elliot, Kevin Fox, Eddy Jadot, John Joseet, Chris Moss, Robert Murray, Stephen Power, Peter Randall, Carlos Reyes-Manzo, Rick Ryscavage, Catherine Shelley, Norman Tanner, and special thanks to Louise Pirouet who did much of the writing.

KEEPING HOPE ALIVE

Who finds refuge in Britain?

Photographs by Carlos Reyes-Manzo

APA

JRS

First published in 1996 by
Andes Press Agency
26 Padbury Court, London, E2 7EH
tel. 0171 613 5417 fax. 0171 739 3159

ISBN 0-9527182-2-7

Design Valeria Baker, Andes Press Agency

Printed by Russell Press Ltd, Nottingham

Cover photo of Kurdish girl in refugee camp in Zakho, Kurdistan
by Carlos Reyes-Manzo

Contents

	Forewords	6
I.	Strangers and Exiles in the Scriptures	11
II.	Refugees in Britain - background	19
III.	Who's who?	31
IV.	Asylum seekers in Britain and Europe today	39
V.	Refusing asylum	47
VI.	The right of appeal	57
VII.	Detention	65
VIII.	Flight: its 'root causes'	71
IX.	The teaching of the Catholic Church	81
X.	Action	89
	Further reading	95
	Acknowledgements	96

Forewords

I. By Cardinal Basil Hume, Archbishop of Westminster

We are all members of the human family, bound together by virtue of our common humanity. The book of Genesis teaches that each one of us is made in the image and likeness of God. Therefore, each individual life, at whatever stage and regardless of his or her circumstances, is of unique worth. When we read in the Scriptures of the persecution of peoples and the tremendous hardships endured by forced migration, we must look to the constancy of God's unfailing mercy and help to those in distress as the basis of our Christian response to this global problem today.

Here, in Britain, much attention has been focussed on the increasing numbers of asylum-seekers. While many are concerned about the well-being of genuine claimants, the problem has also generated fear of an abuse of the system by those migrating for economic reasons only. We must not let selfishness, ignorance and fear prejudice our treatment towards those fleeing conditions of severe repression and persecution. *Keeping Hope Alive* is, indeed, a timely publication by the Jesuit Refugee Service in Britain, seeking to clarify the many factors involved in the whole issue of refugees and asylum-seekers, so enabling the reader to be better informed on all aspects of this serious issue. These include the root causes which have generated the refugee crises; the social and economic considerations which influence attitudes towards refugees; the stringent rules imposed on them on arrival in this country; the numerous difficulties faced in trying to appeal if asylum is refused; and the additional distress suffered through the enforced separation of family members and unlimited stays in detention centres.

As part of its mission, the Church has a duty to concern itself with pressing social issues which touch deeply on human dignity. *Keeping Hope Alive* stresses the importance of the Church's teaching in promoting a positive and compassionate response to the suffering of those vulnerable and marginalised members of our society. Indeed, the Gospels tell us that it is particularly in those who are pushed to the margins that Christ is to be found. This publication is an inspiration to each individual to seek just action towards its resolution and to identify more fully with the suffering of Christ. May we be among those to whom he will say: "I was a stranger and you welcomed me." (Matthew 25:35)

II. By The Very Revd Michael Mayne, Dean of Westminster

I am especially pleased to be asked to write a foreword to a book whose importance is not to be measured by its small size. Whilst *Keeping Hope Alive* is a Roman Catholic initiative, it is broad in its view of the value and dignity of each human being, and it deserves to be read widely by Christians of all traditions.

Hope is central to the Christian gospel, and this book suggests ways of keeping a light burning in what is unquestionably a dark time for refugees and those seeking asylum in Britain. It is also full of information which Christian people need to know if they are to be able to make right judgments and take appropriate action. Statistics, definitions, poems, pictures and prayer: all are a necessary part of a properly informed mind and conscience where fundamental issues of justice and human rights are often at stake.

This is a study which I most warmly recommend.

Sunrise

Sometimes

Sometimes things don't go, after all,
from bad to worse. Some years, muscadel
faces down frost; green thrives; the crops don't fail,
sometimes a man aims high, and all goes well.

A people sometimes will step back from war;
elect an honest man; decide they care
enough, that they can't leave some stranger poor.
Some men become what they were born for.

Sometimes our best efforts do not go
amiss; sometimes we do as we meant to.
The sun will sometimes melt a field of sorrow
that seemed hard frozen: may it happen for you.

Sheenagh Pugh

Kurdish refugees returning home, Zakho, Kurdistan

I. Strangers and Exiles in the Scriptures

There is much in the Bible which is relevant to thinking about how we should treat strangers and refugees. **Migration**, travelling in search of one's true home, the idea of life being a journey, is a familiar metaphor in the Bible and in the Christian tradition. Another biblical theme which is of great importance when thinking about strangers, exiles and refugees is that of **hospitality**.

In the societies which made up the worlds of the Old and New Testaments, as in many non-Western societies today, those who travelled or who moved away from home for any reason were dependent on the hospitality of the people among whom they found themselves. Modern Western travellers who can rely on hotels and telecommunications or organised safari tours may find it hard to realise the absolute necessity of the practice of hospitality in other societies. For us it has too often become an optional extra, and so we are impoverished.

Hospitality is much more than a necessity of travel. It is a sign of friendship, an act of enrichment for both guest and host, an obligation to those who, like us, are made in the image of God, and therefore members of the same worldwide family.

And Judaism and Christianity do not have a monopoly in emphasising the virtue of hospitality. Muslims, Sikhs, Hindus, Buddhists and the followers of many other faiths all recognise the importance of hospitality and the near-sacred responsibility of host to guest.

Hospitality in the Old Testament

- Genesis 18 tells a wonderful story, one of whose themes is hospitality:

  The **Lord** appeared to Abraham by the oaks of Mamre, as he sat at the entrance of his tent in the heat of the day. He looked up and saw three men standing near him. When he saw them, he ran from the tent entrance to meet them, and bowed down to the ground.

  He said, "My lord, if I find favour with you, do not pass by your servant. Let a little water be brought, and wash your feet, and rest yourselves under the tree. Let me bring a little bread, that you may refresh yourselves, and after that you may pass on - since you have come to your servant."

  So they said, "Do as you have said."

  And Abraham hastened into the tent to Sarah, and said, "Make ready quickly three measures of choice flour, knead it, and make cakes."

  Abraham ran to the herd and took a calf, tender and good, and gave it to the servant, who hastened to prepare it. Then he took curds and milk and the calf that he had prepared, and set it before them; and he stood by them under the tree while they ate.

  They said to him, "Where is your wife, Sarah?"

  And he said, "There, in the tent."

  Then one said, "I will surely return to you in due season, and your wife Sarah shall have a son." (Genesis 18:1-10)

Marvellous news! For Abraham was an old man, and Sarah was long past the menopause. Abraham recognised the three travellers as messengers from God, and a son was born to the couple just nine months later as they had promised; a sign that hospitality and God's blessing go together.

"Do not neglect to show hospitality to strangers," enjoins the New Testament writer to the Hebrews, in a reference to this story, "for by doing that some have entertained angels without knowing it." (Hebrews 13: 2)

• Generations later Abraham's descendants found themselves strangers and foreigners in Egypt. They had fled from famine, and were welcomed at first, but eventually fell into destitution and slavery. Their escape from slavery and their wanderings in the desert of Sinai before they settled in Palestine was an experience they have never forgotten. Modern Jews still celebrate Passover each year in commemoration of God's marvellous deliverance.

The suffering of the Hebrew people during their years in Egypt laid on them a moral obligation to be merciful to foreigners, strangers, exiles:

> *"When an alien resides with you in your land, you shall not oppress the alien. The alien who resides with you shall be to you as the citizen among you; you shall love the alien as yourself, for you were aliens in the land of Egypt."* (Leviticus 19:33-4)

This commandment was so important that it is repeated several times over in the Books of the Law, the Pentateuch.

Hospitality in the New Testament

When we come to the New Testament, we find that Jesus himself shared his people's experience of exile.

• St Matthew's gospel tells the story of **The Holy Family's flight into Egypt**. They had to flee to Egypt, leaving home in the dead of night, in order to escape from the crazed paranoia of the tyrant, Herod, who set about the slaughter of a whole generation in order to secure his own power. They stayed there until after Herod's death, when it was safe for them to return home. St Matthew tells this story in order to emphasise Jesus' solidarity with his people: he had even shared symbolically in the exile that the Hebrew people had suffered long before.

• **In his adult life, too,** Jesus suffered homelessness. St Luke records his saying that, though the foxes had dens and birds their nests, he had nowhere to lay his head. (Luke 9:58)

• **Matthew records a parable** Jesus told about the way in which God will finally judge our conduct. We shall be judged, not on the number of times we have attended Mass or the times we have spent in prayer or the number of quiet days or retreats we have made (good though all these things are), but on whether or not it can be said of us:

> **"When I was hungry, you gave me food; when thirsty you gave me drink; when I was a stranger, you took me into your home; when naked you clothed me; when I was ill, you came to my help; when in prison you visited me ... anything you did for one of my brothers here, however humble, you did for me."**
>
> (Matthew 25:34-36, 40)

Unlike our frontiers,
God's frontiers may be crossed
without permit or passport.
There is a frontier I may cross
deep within my heart.
There is a frontier I may cross
as I reach out in concern
to another person's need.
Always I live on the frontier.

Congregational Prayer Fellowship,
CMS Newsletter, July-Sept, 1995.
Slightly adapted.

When the song of the angels is stilled,
when the star in the sky is gone,
when the kings and princes are home,
when the shepherds are back with their flocks,
the work of Christmas begins:
to find the lost,
to heal the broken,
to feed the hungry,
to release the prisoner,
to rebuild the nations,
to bring peace among people,
and make music in the heart.

Anon.

Mother and child in Makalle, Ethiopia 1984

Mother, who heard the child whimper
Beneath the thin blue shawl,
Our aching hearts cry out to thee:
Mother, pray for them all.

A thousand Bethlehems mask dark to night,
The eyes of little friendly homes have lost their light.
Pathetic heaps of poor, dead things are laid aside ...

A latched door swings,
A small bird sings.

Mother, whose sad Egyptian flight preceded all of these,
Guide them in faith beneath familiar stars
Our Lady of the Refugees.

Source Unknown

Diana, exile from Uruguay, and her daughter, South London

II. Refugees in Britain - Background

In the past, **refugees have fled from Britain**. Thankfully this no longer happens. Those who were forced to flee found sanctuary (or asylum to use the modern term) in a number of different countries.

King Edward I of England expelled all **the Jews** from England in 1290, turning them into refugees. A few Jews came back to England when they were expelled from Spain at the end of the fifteenth century, but they did not return in significant numbers until the seventeenth century during the Commonwealth: it was then argued on biblical grounds that Jews ought to be admitted to the country.

Most of those who have been forced to flee from Britain have done so because of religious persecution. At the time of the Reformation, **Catholics** had to flee during the reign of Queen Elizabeth and **Protestants** during the reign of Queen Mary. Later, both **Quakers** and other Nonconformists as well as Catholics fled to America.

In the nineteenth century, extreme economic hardship led to thousands of **Scots** being dispossessed of their land, and of **Irish** leaving for America during the potato famine in their country.

Our main concern here, however, is refugees who have fled to Britain. Various groups of persecuted people have come to Britain as refugees in recent centuries.

Among the refugees who found asylum in Britain were the **Huguenots**, Protestant Christians seeking asylum from persecution in

France in the seventeenth century. Many were skilled silk weavers and silversmiths whose products can be seen in the British Museum (silver) and the Victoria and Albert Museum (silks). Through their skills they contributed significantly to the economy. They have been fully integrated into British society for a long time.

At the time of the French Revolution, **Catholics** who fled the violence were welcomed into Britain, and the arrival of priests among the émigrés was one of the factors which led to the legalising of Catholic worship in England again.

Jewish people, and people of other persecuted minorities such as the Roma from Eastern Europe, entered Britain from the late nineteenth century onward, and from Germany and Austria in the 1930s and 1940s when they fled the Nazi regime. Some arrived with considerable wealth; others set out with nothing and made their way by hard work and supporting one another through difficult periods of readjustment. Some brought banking, financial and managerial skills, and among those who came to Britain there were also scholars and writers. A number have become MPs and members of governments. Several have won Nobel prizes in the sciences. Perhaps the most famous Jewish refugee was Albert Einstein.

> In spite of the contribution Jews have made to British life, there have been outbreaks of anti-Semitism from time to time, and these seem to be on the increase again in Europe recently. Many Jews have retained a strong sense of their Jewish identity whether or not they are religiously observant.

The largest single contingent of refugees ever to arrive on British shores was the group of four thousand **Basque children** during the 1930s who were sent away from the horrors of the Civil War then raging in Spain. In the light of current events, it is interesting to note that the British Government gave its reluctant permission for the children to come - with the stipulation that no public finance would ever be made available to support them. None ever was.

Refugees from Communism in Eastern Europe form another group of people who have found asylum in Britain from persecution. They were usually highly appreciative of the freedom they gained by coming to the West, and most fitted easily into British life. They were seen as proof of

Communist repression, and an object lesson to those Britons who supported the Communist Party and admired Eastern Bloc-type socialism.

> Among these refugees were Poles who had fought with the allies during World War II and then found themselves unable to return when the USSR overran Poland.

The ideological background to refugee crises affects how easily governments will grant refugee status. For instance, predominantly capitalist governments quickly recognised refugees from communism. But the UK, Europe and the USA were much more reluctant to accept refugees from right-wing, capitalist governments in the 1970s and 80s such as those in Chile, Argentina, El Salvador, Nicaragua and Guatemala.

In 1972 some 27,000 **British Asians from Uganda** had to be admitted to Britain suddenly when the dictator Idi Amin expelled them, giving them 90 days in which to leave. These were not refugees, in that they had British citizenship, and were being very slowly admitted to Britain anyhow, but the manner of their expulsion put them in a similar position to refugees.

> The arrival of the Asians from Uganda divided the British people. On the one hand, the voluntary agencies, including the churches, and many individuals and local groups, welcomed these suddenly dispossessed people. Others, however, were alarmed and angry at the sudden influx of people of a different culture at a time when there was growing concern about housing shortages and unemployment.

Many of the educated displaced British Asians who had lived in Ugandan towns quite quickly found their way into employment. Others, however, who were less Westernised, remained in poverty, some permanently. The older generation often failed to learn English (there was no official provision made for this).

The Asians expelled from Uganda included Muslims, Hindus, Sikhs and Catholic Christians (who were originally from Goa), and many have retained their traditional allegiances, though some of the younger generation are becoming secularised and abandoning traditional customs. By and large, however, the British Asians from Uganda have done well.

> The Asians from Uganda are usually lumped together in the popular imagination with people from **Pakistan** and **India**. These people are not refugees but were recruited immediately after World War II to help alleviate an acute labour shortage. They have been in Britain some twenty years longer. They arrived together with a large number of people from the Caribbean recruited for the same reason: acute labour shortages after the war in public transport and elsewhere, which were threatening Britain's economic recovery. The vast majority of people of Asian and Afro-Caribbean origin are now British citizens, and a whole generation has been born here.

In the mid-1970s those accepted from Communist countries included **'Boat-people' from Vietnam**. TV showed pictures of little boats almost swamped at sea whose occupants were sometimes rescued by British ships. Many went to Hong Kong, but the government decided that Britain should take a quota of these, and special arrangements were made to admit them.

A government campaign prepared people to accept them by making much of our tradition of providing safety for people who were suffering persecution. However, it was left to the voluntary agencies, including the churches, to help them to settle here. Great efforts were made, but no one would claim that these were fully successful. In particular, provisions for learning English were patchy. It was a long time before some people found employment: some never have, although many Vietnamese have since been highly successful in business and education.

In more recent times, and especially in the 1990s, those who seek asylum in Britain are coming mainly from Africa, the Indian subcontinent and the Middle East, and are fleeing rather different kinds of tyrannies, though no less vicious ones.

The increase in numbers seeking asylum from 1989 onwards is partly connected with the collapse of communism. This led to a surging demand throughout much of the world for greater freedom and democracy. 'People power' had worked in East Germany, Czechoslovakia, Hungary, South Korea, and the Philippines, and democratic governments were installed. At a slightly later stage long-established rulers suddenly found themselves out of power in Zambia and Malawi. Elsewhere, ruthless regimes became yet more ruthless in an attempt to ensure that they, too, were not overthrown.

At the same time people's 'tolerance threshhold' for repression and deprivation was lowered. As had happened in East Germany in 1989 where repression had led to economic stagnation, people started to try to escape the deprivation they were being forced to endure. It is often difficult to disentangle political repression on the one hand, and economic deprivation on the other. Economic deprivation may actually be used as a tool of repression as well as simply resulting from it.

In the 1980s many Eritreans, Ethiopians and Somalis were accepted in the UK partly because of the complete devastation in their countries, not because they were all individually persecuted.

A recent study, *The Settlement of Refugees in Britain*, conducted for the Home Office, notes that:

> "The majority of asylum-seekers come with substantial work and educational qualifications, the bulk of which are under-utilised, to their chagrin and the country's general loss.
>
> "...There was a high rate of physical and psychological stress, largely consequent upon their past experiences that led individuals to seek asylum, and because of separation from their families. Virtually no help is being provided to help them cope with these difficulties."

As well as expressing the need for the general public to be better informed about refugees, the Report says: "Statutory agencies, and especially social landlords, need to ensure that their practice discourages harassment". It comments on the important part played by refugee community groups. Without their support, the Report suggests, "it is difficult to see how many of the newcomers would have been able to survive".

The rise in refugee numbers alarms Western governments.

> The main reason for this alarm in Britain is probably economic. Unemployment is high and unlikely to come down quickly, and there would be an outcry if people believed their jobs were being taken by newcomers. High unemployment means that social security is costing many millions. The government does not want to see this bill rise further by having to pay social security to asylum-seekers, even though the amounts involved are only a tiny percentage of the total.
>
> A second reason concerns the fear of a backlash against highly visible minorities. It is feared that British tolerance would be strained by a further influx of people whose skin colour made them highly visible. This argument lays the blame for poor race relations on 'being black' rather than on white intolerance.

This alarm is misguided as regards the UK. For many years the number of people leaving the country has been greater than the number entering it. Governments are tending to confuse immigration policies with asylum and the need for protection.

There are other reasons why refugees in the 1990s are less welcome than those who came earlier. It is not only a fear of numbers. Today's asylum-seekers are not, for the most part, fleeing from communist regimes, so they serve no particular political purpose. Indeed, as has sometimes been the case in the past, Britain may find herself called upon to give asylum to people fleeing from her allies or her valued trading partners.

> Refugees from the Kurdish minority in Turkey are examples of this phenomenon. Turkey is pro-West, a NATO ally, and is seen as a bastion of moderation against more extreme Middle Eastern governments. Britain has, as a result, been extremely cautious about angering Turkey by accepting Kurdish refugees.

Refugees are also less welcome for reasons concerning our export trade. For instance, many repressive Middle Eastern governments buy huge amounts of arms and other goods from Britain. The **arms export trade** is so important to the economy that the government is reluctant to do anything which might annoy such states and lead them to buy their arms elsewhere.

In 1996 the British Government refused asylum to a Saudi dissident as a refugee because to do so would endanger armaments exports. However, the courts ruled that he could not be removed to a country where he would not be safe, so he had to be allowed to remain in Britain.

Mrs Sadako Ogata, the UN High Commissioner for Refugees, has said repeatedly that refugee crises will only be solved by dealing with their 'root causes'. If people face intolerable conditions at home, they will seek sanctuary elsewhere. In saying this, Mrs Ogata is addressing not only those governments which repress their citizens, but all governments. We all have a responsibility to deter governments which repress their citizens and drive them into becoming refugees.

Maria and Josef Nawara

Their Experiences as Refugees in Britain

My name is Maria Antonlin Nawara. I was born in Santurce Ortuelle, Bilbao in the Basque country, Spain. I had a very happy childhood and was twelve years old when the Civil War started in 1936; from then on nothing was ever the same. My father and 18 year old brother went to fight on the side of the Republicans with sticks - all the Republican Army was ill-equipped. The rest of the family had to manage the best we could. We spent nearly all day in a tunnel which was our air-raid shelter.

The following year, May 1937, the Basque government organised the evacuation of 4000 Basque children, the biggest in history to the UK; my young brother, sister and myself were among them. When the Nationalists occupied the North of Spain my father and oldest brother went into hiding; they later tried to go across the Pyrenees to France. Unfortunately, due to a poisoned foot, father had to return and stayed hidden for three years, helped by a republican doctor who saved his leg. My brother managed to get over to France and later on he went to Chile.

In 1949 my younger brother left the UK for Chile, the aim being to unite all the family in Chile, but it was not to be. My mother and 19 year old sister were tortured for months by the Guardia Civil, who wanted to know the whereabouts of my eldest brother. One day a letter arrived from Chile: as soon as they read it the Guardia Civil did not bother them any more. My father came home and he too was left alone.

While Franco was in power my eldest brother could not enter Spain without risking being arrested. He died in 1969, my father in 1976 and mam in 1978 after a long illness. My two sisters also died eighteen years later within one year of each other in the village of Santurce Ortuelle. My young brother is still in Chile, he has been to Spain and the UK many times. I settled in the UK and have lived in Brixton for the last 30 years.

My name is Josef Nawara. Like so many other Poles, my life was completely changed with the advent of the Second World War. I come from the Katowice in Upper Silesia, which then was only a few kilometres from the German border. Three days after the war started, the Germans marched in, and the world I knew as a child came to an end. When the

Germans occupied Silesia, they started classifying the inhabitants into Germans, Poles, Jews and Gypsies. It meant the Jews and Gypsies went to ghettos in occupied Poland. Silesia was incorporated into Germany. Being classified as a Pole meant you had no rights to education. The aim was to keep us as unskilled labour. At work we had 15% deducted in addition to income tax. Ration cards were reduced.

In 1942 the Germans reclassified young men born in 1926 and after as Germans, so they could be pressed into the German army. The irony was that after having been regarded and treated as a sub-human for three years, I became in 1943 a German soldier, but not trusted enough to be sent to the Eastern Front. After the Allied landing in Normandy in June 1944, I went over the lines to the Americans. As a P.O.W. I was segregated with Czechs, Yugoslavs, Lithuanians, Italians and other nationalities.

On arrival in Britain the Poles and Czechs joined their respective national armies. The end of hostilities brought more problems for us. First the British withdrew the recognition of the Polish Government in Exile, and recognised the Communist-led Government in Poland. Next we were disarmed and the army became the Polish Resettlement Corps.

The Polish authorities insisted on our returning to Poland, but the British left the choice of going back or staying in Britain to us. In spite of threats of withdrawing our Polish nationality on the part of the Communists, a very great number of us elected to remain as stateless under British Protection. After the demobilization from the Polish Resettlement Corps I moved to London where I met my wife. Not having a passport I experienced a great many difficulties in travelling abroad so I became a naturalized British Subject. It did not change me; I still remained a refugee and a foreigner.

By the rivers of Babylon, there we sat down and
there we wept when we remembered Zion.

On the willows there we hung up our harps.
For there our captors asked us for songs,
and our tormentors asked for mirth, saying
"Sing us one of the songs of Zion!"

How could we sing the Lord's song
in a foreign land?

If I forget you, O Jerusalem,
let my right hand wither!

Let my tongue cleave to the roof of my mouth,
if I do not remember you,
if I do not set Jerusalem above my highest joy.

Psalm 137:1-6

Helping to Keep Hope Alive

The Refugee Council

The Refugee Council is the largest provider of services to refugees and asylum-seekers in the UK. It also helps to promote refugees' rights, both in the UK and abroad.

Through its *Settlement Division*, the Refugee Council helps newly-arrived asylum-seekers who may be penniless and possess nothing but the clothes they stand up in.

The *Advice and Referral Team* offers help on immigration status, housing, benefits, health, education and employment. This is a walk-in service.

The *Refugee Training and Employment Centre* helps some 1,000 refugees and asylum-seekers each year with training and employment.

Other advice groups such as Citizens Advice Bureaux are assisted by the *Refugee Advisors Support Unit* which runs a telephone advice line and sends out up-to-date information regularly.

A *Community Development Team* assists refugee community groups, and a *National Development Team* supports the regional Refugee Councils and other organisations outside London.

Other specialised activities include the *Children's Division* and its Panel of Advisors for Unaccompanied Refugee Children. The Refugee Council runs two hostels, Korczak House which can accommodate unaccompanied children on arrival and Agnew House, a home for elderly refugees.

The establishment of a *Day Centre* and a *Night Shelter* are among the Refugee Council's responses to the loss of social security benefit by most asylum-seekers as a result of the 1996 Asylum Act.

The *International Division* of the Refugee Council provides a forum for British Non-Governmental Organisations working among refugees all over the world. Four Regional Committees (Africa, Asia, Middle East, Latin America) meet regularly. The Refugee Council aims to highlight problems of refugee care and protection around the world in collaboration with NGOs, to draw attention to the root causes of the refugee flows into the UK, and to run special information and other projects.

Bethnal Green, London

III. Who's Who?

'Refugees', 'immigrants', 'asylum-seekers', 'economic migrants', 'illegals': all these words are bandied about, and sometimes used wrongly in the press. But what exactly do they mean?

Immigrants

The word 'immigrant' is often used, colloquially and mistakenly, to refer to people of African, Afro-Caribbean and Asian origin. Many people in these communities have been born here, and dislike being referred to in this way.

A quite different meaning is used when official statistics are being compiled:

- For UK **census** purposes, an immigrant is anyone who was not in Britain a year ago and who is now.
- **The United Nations** definition of an immigrant counts anyone who goes to another state and intends to remain for a year or more.

Immigration figures compiled on this basis include, for instance:

- British citizens who have been working abroad
- EU citizens taking up posts in Britain

- Japanese businessmen setting up manufacturing firms in Britain
- the foreign wives of British servicemen who got engaged while serving overseas
- children born to British parents overseas
- American professors on temporary secondments
- wealthy Hong Kong businessmen with £750,000 to invest in Treasury Bonds, who thus acquire the right to live in this country.

The immigration statistics also include those recognised as 'refugees' or those given 'exceptional leave to remain' (see below) for humanitarian reasons each year (about 5,000 people in 1995). A very small number of Black and Asian people are allowed in to join their families who are already settled here.

Emigrants

The Home Office does not keep statistics of those who leave the country. As a result, the impression is sometimes given that there is a continual addition to the population through immigration. This is not so.

The European Union Statistical Service compiles statistics according to the United Nations formula. They found that in 1992 216,000 people immigrated into Britain whilst 227,000 people emigrated from the country. *The Daily Telegraph*, which reported this, went on to say:

> "These figures suggest that tales of a flood-tide of immigrants have been exaggerated ... Expressed as a percentage of total population, Britain's rate of immigration is among the lowest in Europe, running at less than 0.5% per year. It is exceeded in Belgium, Denmark, Germany, Ireland, Luxembourg, Holland and Sweden."

The article continued by saying that some people seemed keen:

> "to perpetuate the myth that Britain is being invaded by hordes of poor, illiterate people who are sponging off the welfare system. But [the Office of Population Censuses & Surveys] report from 1993 tells a different story, saying that many people entering Britain come

'only for a short period of time to work or study before returning home again. Many of these people are highly skilled workers; they are the typical migrants of the present day.'"

Many refugees eventually return home. Over the past 15 years refugees from Zimbabwe, Chile, Argentina, Namibia and South Africa have returned home when new governments brought an end to persecution. Most of those who seek refuge in Britain want nothing more than to be able to return home, and many do so as soon as they believe it to be safe. Understandably, those who have lived here a long time and whose children have grown up here and been educated in the British system are less likely to want to do so.

Illegal Immigrants

An illegal immigrant (a term much misunderstood and misused) is someone who:

- has entered or has sought to enter the UK without leave (i.e. without a valid visa or entry permit), or who has overstayed his permission to be here.
- has entered the UK whilst a deportation order was in force prohibiting his re-entry.
- has entered by deceiving an immigration officer, e.g. by using a false passport or by not revealing the full facts of his situation.

Someone seeking asylum may unwittingly find him or herself in one of these categories.

> Because a person is 'illegal' for immigration purposes, it does not mean she or he is a criminal. Indeed, illegal immigrants are often the victims of criminal racketeers who prey on vulnerable people and extort their last resources with the promise of a new future.

Asylum-seekers

Those who apply to the Home Office for asylum are termed 'asylum-seekers' while decisions on their cases are pending. The only right an asylum-seeker has is the right not to be removed from Britain while his or her case is being decided.

Refugees

This term is used in common speech to mean anyone who goes from one place to another to seek relief from adverse circumstances. In law, however, the term 'refugee' has a very precise meaning.

> A refugee is anyone who "...owing to a well-founded fear of persecution for reasons of race, religion, nationality, membership of a particular social group or political opinion, is outside the country of his nationality and is unable, or owing to such fear, unwilling to avail himself of the protection of that country...". (UN Convention Relating to the Status of Refugees, 1951, Article 1)

Article 14 of the **UN Universal Declaration of Human Rights** gives everyone the right: **"To seek and enjoy in other countries asylum from persecution"**. It does not give the right to find asylum. The host government has the responsibility of deciding whether a person should be recognised as a refugee as defined above. The burden of proof lies on the person seeking asylum, and in the West it is increasingly difficult for a person to prove that he or she should be recognised as a refugee.

Exceptional leave to remain for humanitarian reasons

Some people who seek asylum in Britain are not recognised as refugees but are given this status rather than full refugee status under the Convention.

Those with Exceptional Leave to Remain do not have the same rights as Refugees. They have to renew their status from time to time, and therefore live in fear that they may one day be refused permission to remain. In particular, they do not have the right to be joined by their spouses and dependent children. They may begin applying to be joined by their families at the end of four years from the time they were granted Exceptional Leave to Remain. By that time, some of their children may have reached the age of 18 and so be ineligible to join them.

Until recently, large numbers of those who applied for asylum were given this Exceptional Leave status. Since the 1993 Asylum and Immigration Act came into force, the Home Office is giving this status more and more sparingly.

Nostalgias

Time is dancing, singing,
crossing abysses,
weaving nostalgias,
imprisoning memories,
sowing sadness along its path.

Here you hold me prisoner
of eternal melancholies.

Nostalgia, you who bring illusions
of distant lands.

Nostalgia for my beloved land,
for bread fragrant of eucalyptus
kneaded by the white hands
of the mother
of your absent son.

I want to return to the maternal bay,
to anchor my phantom boat
in the blue Pacific waters;
the ancient port is waiting.

Carlos Reyes-Manzo

Sou Huoy Lam

Her Experience as a Refugee in Britain

Sou Huoy Lam left her home in Cambodia in the 1980s to seek asylum after her parents were killed when she felt herself to be endangered too. By this time the Pol Pot regime had ended, and the refugee camps in Thailand had been closed to newcomers, and Huoy had to sneak into a camp when the guards were not looking. To reach the camp she had to work her way through minefields.

Houy's brother, who escaped three years earlier, was fortunate enough to be resettled in the United States. However, she and some others from the camp managed to get passports and a flight to Europe. But no country was prepared to admit them, and they found themselves "in orbit" for 50 hours, being flown from one country to another.

Finally they were returned to Singapore, where it seemed they would be removed back to Thailand where they expected to be put in prison. Huoy's companion, Huy Lim, became so desperate at the thought of this that he slashed his wrists.

When everyone else had refused to accept Huoy, she was admitted to Britain because the plane she was flying on was British.

That was 10 years ago, and Huoy has not seen her brother since 1980. One of their last surviving relatives now lives in China, and they are planning a meeting together there.

Meanwhile Huoy has completed a degree in computing, and is using her skills in a job helping other refugees.

Helping to Keep Hope Alive

The Medical Foundation for the Care of Victims of Torture

The Medical Foundation's help for tortured asylum-seekers is not limited to treatment as the following story shows.

Felix and Anjila (not their real names) are from the Ivory Coast. They arrived in Britain, distressed and frightened, at the beginning of February 1996. Felix had just been released from prison and still bore some very obvious marks from his ordeal such as severe bruising to his head. His wife, Anjila, had suffered a miscarriage just prior to his release and was still bleeding when they arrived in England.

Like many asylum-seekers, they did not state their intentions at their port of entry but two days later, and as a result are now not entitled to receive social security benefits. Felix and Anjila became one of the first couples to fall foul of the new benefits regulations which came into force on 5 February 1996.

They went to the Refugee Council for assistance, and the Refugee Council contacted the Medical Foundation for emergency help. Three volunteers, a doctor, interpreter and medical secretary, were then hastily located on a Saturday morning and asked to come to the Foundation's headquarters in Grafton Road, Kentish Town as a matter of urgency. They then spent several hours with Felix, gently drawing out his story and examining him for signs of torture. The Foundation referred Anjila to a specialist clinic for much needed medical treatment.

The Medical Foundation's report formed the basis of a High Court case where it was judged that the couple should be given temporary housing by Southwark Council because of their obvious vulnerability pending a test case on their right to permanent housing.

Demonstration outside the Home Office, London 1994

IV. Asylum-seekers in Britain and Europe today

1. Asylum in Britain

The Home Office claims to operate a 'firm but fair' **immigration policy**. The Government (1996) says it is committed to fulfilling the United Kingdom's obligations under the 1951 United Nations Convention on Refugees. It claims that many asylum-seekers are 'bogus', and has therefore drawn up new legislation which it hopes will deter 'bogus' asylum-seekers.

The changes in UK policy of the 1990s have been challenged by the **United Nations Commission for Refugees (UNHCR)**. The UNHCR wrote a memorandum to the government about its plans to remove social security benefits from many asylum-seekers. In this they stated their belief that the rise in asylum claims was not simply the result of economic migrants seeking a better life in the West. They believed that a more rational explanation was that global conflict on an unprecedented scale was producing the increased flow of refugees. They went on to say that "refugee recognition rates must be analysed with considerable caution":

> "A country's recognition rate of refugees may more often reflect the narrowness or liberalness of that state's application of the refugee definition than the legitimacy or otherwise of individual claims.

"There are dangerous shortcomings in any assumption that the low refugee recognition rate in the United Kingdom is evidence of the extent of 'bogus claimants' ...

"These unsound assumptions are frequently cited as justification for further restrictive measures. For example, a narrow application of the refugee definition and tighter grants on exceptional leave to remain will reduce the number of successful applicants. The lower figures are then tendentiously used as evidence that 'bogus' claims are increasing, thereby justifying further restrictive measures. We believe there are many dangers in such a self-justificatory and circular analysis."

It may be useful at this point to look at some statistics on asylum. (See Tables 1 and 2). The source of all statistics relating to the United Kingdom is the Home Office which has responsibility for asylum and immigration. Statistics for other European countries come from the European Council on Refugees and Exiles who again use information provided by governments.

UK Asylum Applications

Table 1: Asylum-seekers in the UK 1990-1996

Year	Number of asylum applications received	Number of decisions reached by the Home Office	Number granted Refugee Status and Exceptional Leave to Remain		Refusals of Refugee Status and Exceptional Leave to remain	
1990 a	26,205	4,023	3,430	83%	705	17%
1991	44,840	6,075	2,695	44%	3,380	56% b
1992	24,605	34,900	16,435	47%	18,465	53%
1993	22,370	23,405	12,715	55%	10,690	45%
1994	32,380	20,990	4,490	21%	16,500	79%
1995	43,965	27,005	5,671	21%	21,334	79%
1996 c	(9,315)	(9,260)	(1,760)	19%	(7,500)	81%

a In the years 1984-1989 the average rate of refusal was c. 20%.

b These figures are inflated by the inclusion of a large number of people refused on technicalities. It is uncertain how many of the refusals represented 'real' cases.

c Figures for January-March only.

The total number of people given asylum during the whole of this period was 56,363. This is in a population of c. 56,000,000.

Table 2: The top ten countries from which people sought asylum in the UK in 1995

Country	Number of asylum-seekers	Number of decisions made	Number given Refugee Status		Number given Exceptional Leave to Remain		Percentage Refused
Nigeria	5,825	2,630	0	0%	78	3%	97%
India	3,225	2,010	0	0%	40	2%	98%
Pakistan	2,915	1,675	7	1%	17	1%	98%
Sri Lanka	2,070	1,340	27	2%	91	7%	91%
Ghana	1,915	1,975 a	0	0%	20	1%	99%
Algeria	1,865	745	15	2%	10	1%	97%
Turkey	1,820	995	49	5%	40	4%	91%
Former Yugoslavia	1,565	1,860 a	279	15%	744	40%	45%
Tanzania	1,535	365	0	0%	0	0%	100%
Kenya	1,395	515	0	0%	15	3%	97%
Somalia	1,040	2,400	24	1%	2,208	92%	7%

a The Home Office has a huge backlog of undecided cases, and the extra cases will be from this backlog.

In trying to evaluate the government's policy, let us look at **who seeks asylum in Britain**:

1. Most asylum-seekers come from countries where there is severe repression, large-scale abuse of human rights, and perhaps also civil war.

2. They often come from countries where famine and economic hardship result from repression.

3. Many asylum-seekers come from countries where people's hopes of democracy have been dashed. Nigeria's military rulers have refused to give up power, Zaire's President Mobutu has repeatedly succeeded in preventing promised elections and blocking promised moves towards democracy.

4. Others come from regimes which reject any suggestion of democracy. The present Muslim extremist government of Sudan is just one example

of this. A number of Middle Eastern governments are totalitarian and often unpredictable.

5. In many of the countries from which asylum-seekers come to Britain, government is close to breaking down, and the army and other 'security forces' are out of control and prey on the population. The government may be either unable or unwilling to prevent this.

2. Asylum in Europe

In recent years, many member states of the European Union have responded to the growth of concern about immigration by trying to restrict both immigration and asylum. Governments are worried by the growth of unemployment, which eats up huge amounts of taxpayers' money in social security payments. This has led to the emergence of what has come to be known as 'fortress-Europe'. This is a Europe which has a high wall all round it of strict immigration controls. These are intended to safeguard the living standards of those inside the protective walls, by keeping out destitute 'economic migrants'.

These policies have been worked out by Home Affairs Ministers or senior civil servants meeting in secret. Not even the Office of the UN High Commissioner for Refugees has been admitted to the discussions on policy-making about refugees. The EU member states are also seeking to standardise their policies and practices. The British Government tried to justify its decision to introduce benefit cuts for asylum-seekers which came into force early in 1996 by appealing to the policies in other European States. Many voluntary organisations working with refugees, including the European Council on Refugees and Exiles (ECRE) and the [British] Refugee Council fear that standardising asylum rights in Europe will mean reducing them to the lowest common denominator. The General Secretary of ECRE fears that refugees are being "defined out of existence".

Table 3: Numbers of people seeking asylum in the European Union

Year	Number
1992	700,000
1993	550,000
1994	320,000

The numbers dropped as the controls on asylum-seekers have grown ever more strict.

Table 4: Numbers of asylum-seekers 1993-1995 in the European Union

(Prior to the 1990s the number of asylum-seekers coming to the United Kingdom was much smaller in proportion to her population than in a number of other European countries. In the 1990s the United Kingdom has 'caught up' with the rest of Europe.)

Country	Population	1993	1994	1995
Germany	78,000,000	322,842	127,210	129,517 a
Italy	57,100,000	1,646	1,766	1,732
United Kingdom	55,900,000	22,370	32,380	43,965
France	53,655,000	27,564	26,044	20,170
Spain	37,480,000	12,615	11,992	4,429
Netherlands	14,200,000	35,399	52,576	29,528 a
Portugal	9,900,000	1,659	614	322
Belgium	9,860,000	26,882	14,353	11,409 a
Greece	9,300,000	789	1,227	1,318 a
Sweden	8,320,000	37,581	18,640	9,046 a
Austria	7,503,000	4,744	4,520	5,920 a
Denmark	5,132,000	14,347	6,654	5,112 a
Finland	4,776,000	2,032	836	756 a
Ireland	3,420,000	91	355	424
Luxembourg	364,000	225	165	155

a Countries with a larger number of asylum-seekers than the United Kingdom in proportion to the size of their population.

It is not fully understood why numbers seeking asylum have risen in some countries and fallen in others.

Helping to Keep Hope Alive

Amnesty International

Amnesty International has provided the following information about its work for refugees and asylum-seekers.

Inaugurated in 1961, Amnesty International is a worldwide voluntary movement that works to prevent some of the gravest violations by governments of people's fundamental human rights. Amnesty International has more that 1,100,000 members in 150 countries, and is financed by subscriptions and donations from its worldwide membership with no funds being sought or accepted from governments.

Amnesty International's work for the protection of refugees and asylum-seekers derives directly from its prisoner-related concerns. The organisation opposes the forcible return of any person to a country where they might reasonably be expected to be imprisoned as a prisoner of conscience, subjected to torture, 'disappearance' or execution.

In recent years, many governments have become less committed to the fundamental principles of refugee law which have been developed by the international community; some governments seem more concerned with limiting the number of asylum-seekers who reach their borders than with providing proper asylum procedures; and there is little focus on stopping the human rights abuses which cause refugee movements. Amnesty International monitors the policy and asylum procedures of governments to ensure that they are adequate to identify refugees at risk. The organisation's concerns extend to the asylum policy and practice of the European Union and its harmonisation of asylum policies within the member states, drafted by an obscure group of EU home affairs officials from which the main elements of domestic legislation stem.

The organisation provides country of origin information to lawyers and refugee practitioners working on behalf of asylum-seekers and refugees both at the initial stages of an asylum application and at the appeal stage. The Amnesty International refugee officers around the world share information and join together to campaign on refugee issues of concern to the organisation both regionally and globally.

Agar Chol and Sara Chol

Their Experiences as Refugees in Britain

Agar Chol is originally from southern Sudan. There has been an armed conflict for many years between the mainly Arab and Muslim north of Sudan and the south. The peoples of the south are black Africans who are mainly Christians or followers of traditional African beliefs. As a result of the conflict, many southerners have been displaced to the north or across the borders of Sudan into neighbouring countries. The conflict escalated in 1989 when a hardline Muslim government seized power in Khartoum.

Agar was studying for a postgraduate degree at London University when the situation for southerners deteriorated to such an extent that he applied for asylum here. He was recognised as a Convention refugee and his wife, Sara, and her younger sister were able to join him.

Agar and Sara now have four young children. They are with him in Britain, but other members of Agar's family are dispersed in southern Sudan and in Egypt, and they all depend to some extent on the financial help that Agar is able to send to them.

Agar has recently returned from Somaliland. This is the northern part of Somalia which has broken away from the rest of the country and is now peaceful. There, he has been helping to resettle Somalis who have been able to return home from Ethiopia where they had fled during the recent upheavals in Somalia.

Agar applied for asylum when he was already in Britain for another reason, namely as a student. Anyone who now applies "in-country" as he did has no right to social security benefits, and may find themselves completely destitute.

Names have been changed.

Lo Cañas, secret detention and torture centre during Pinochet's military regime, Santiago, Chile

V. Refusing Asylum

Why are people refused asylum? We set out here some of the hurdles which confront those who ask for protection from persecution.

1. They must persuade the Home Office that their claim is credible

People are usually refused because the Home Office, and the adjudicators, to whom asylum-seekers may appeal if the Home Office refuses them asylum, decide that the person's story is 'not credible'. Yet assessing credibility is extremely difficult, as some adjudicators admit.

The rules say that an asylum-seeker must make "full and prompt disclosure" of all relevant facts, and if they fail to do so, it will count against them. But when people are interviewed soon after arrival, they may still be frightened, tired, confused, and distrustful of anyone in authority. They may, as a result, give **a muddled and incomplete account of the reasons for seeking asylum**. A confused story, or one that has to be altered or amplified later, is likely to be found not credible. Under the new legislation the majority of asylum-seekers will be interviewed directly upon arrival, and this worries lawyers and the refugee agencies who assist people to claim asylum.

Even small discrepancies may count against someone. For instance, one asylum-seeker said in an interview that she "went to" the

one asylum-seeker said in an interview that she "went to" the military barracks to look for her husband, and in another she said she was "taken to" the barracks. The discrepancy was taken as evidence of untruthfulness and was said to undermine her credibility. Small discrepancies over dates are also penalised even years after the event.

Some of those who are most in need of protection are those who have suffered **torture**. They may find it particularly difficult to give a full account of what has happened. The memory of torture is sometimes deeply humiliating and the suffering very great. People who have experienced such suffering sometimes cannot bring themselves to talk about it at all except to a skilled therapist or counsellor with whom they have built up a relationship of trust. This may take a long time. But if they add to their original story at a later date, this may be held to undermine their credibility.

There are sometimes elements of an asylum-seeker's story that the Home Office and the adjudicator find too strange to accept as credible. This may be because **a different culture** is not properly understood by the Home Office and the adjudicators. And refugees may have experienced **strange events** which are bizarre indeed by the standards of life in the West, but are nevertheless true.

2. They must apply for asylum at the 'right' time

Yet another reason why people may be refused is that they applied for asylum at **the wrong time**. One way of escaping from hardship in one's own country is to go abroad for a time until the situation improves. But sometimes the situation does not improve or gets worse, so just before the person is due to return, he or she makes an application for asylum. But the rules say that you should apply immediately you think you are endangered, and that it will count against you if you do not.

And there are two further snags regarding the **timing** of one's asylum application. First, it is increasingly difficult to buy an air fare without full documentation, so if possible, people seeking asylum will get a visa. But, if they are admitted to Britain on a visitor's visa and they pass through the immigration controls, and then apply for asylum after finding out how to go about this, even if they do so after only a day or so, they will

seekers will apply as they pass through the immigration controls, and if people do not do so, it will count against them. And, secondly, such people will be disadvantaged because in February 1996 the government removed from them the right to social security benefits. They may, therefore, find themselves destitute. Social security may now only be paid to people who apply for asylum to an immigration officer in the port of arrival.

3. They must prove that they have suffered the 'right kind' of persecution

For instance, people who flee from **civil war** are not considered to fulfil the requirements of the UN Convention on Refugees for that reason alone, even though they may have been displaced by the fighting.

> As a result of a recent European Union decision, states will be able to avoid recognising as refugees people persecuted by **'non state agents'** such as rebel groups or extremist organisations. Their governments may be unwilling or unable to protect them, but asylum-seekers may find this very difficult to prove. The Office of the UN High Commissioner for Refugees considers this a very dangerous precedent. Refugees from Sudan, Algeria, Turkey and Sri Lanka, for instance, could be adversely affected by this decision.

4. They must not have changed planes or stopped over *en route* to the United Kingdom

The UN Convention on Refugees says nothing about which country a person should seek asylum in. But many Western countries have decided that asylum should be sought in the **first safe country** the person reaches. If someone who already has relatives in Britain is forced to flee, and cannot get a direct flight to Britain but changes planes in, say, Amsterdam or Paris, the British authorities will try to return the person to Amsterdam or Paris. Only if a husband or wife is trying to join their spouse, or a parent their dependent children, are they likely to be allowed to remain, and not necessarily even then.

The first 'safe' country through which someone has passed *en route* is, awkwardly enough, called the **third** country! Cases where people are

awkwardly enough, called the **third** country! Cases where people are removed to such countries are called 'safe third country removals'. Unfortunately, some people removed to safe third countries have simply been sent by them straight back to the countries from which they had fled.

The Dublin Convention, agreed among a number of European countries, seeks to set out the rules about which country has the responsibility for dealing with an asylum claim if there is any doubt about this. Because this is not part of European Union law, an aggrieved person cannot take a case to the European Court of Justice.

In a submission to the government the UNHCR stated:

> "UNHCR is of the opinion that there can be no automatic or reliable assumption that simply because an asylum-seeker passed through another EU state ... *en route* to the United Kingdom, the country is 'safe' against *refoulement* [i.e. forcible repatriation], whether directly or indirectly ..."

The UNHCR went on to point out that, in the 14 months from September 1994 to December 1995, they had monitored all decisions made by the adjudicators in cases where an asylum-seeker had appealed against being sent back to a safe third country. In 39% of the cases, the adjudicators had decided that it was NOT safe to return a person there.

However, as a result of the 1996 Asylum and Immigration Act, safe third country cases will only have a right of appeal **after** they have been sent away from the UK. As the UNHCR says, this

> "... may well render the *de jure* right of appeal quite nugatory."

In other words, the right of appeal is rendered virtually worthless.

The refusal rate

Until 1993 only about 20% of those who applied for asylum were rejected. Most applicants were given exceptional leave to remain and a small per-

when the new Asylum and Immigration Appeals Act came into force, all that changed. The **refusal rate** now stands at over 80% and is rising. The percentage recognised as Convention refugees has dropped to a fraction of what it was. Refugee agencies believe that very much harsher conditions for acceptance are now being operated.

Of course, there are some people who claim asylum, but who are rightly refused. It is recognised that States have a right and a duty to control immigration in certain respects. People who are refused asylum need help to enable them to return. Although not refugees, they may have no means left to start anew in their country of origin. They may try to stay illegally, though some would prefer to return home if they could be helped to do so. The Red Cross and other agencies have discussed ways of easing the return of families. This would help to ease the fear Western governments have about 'back-door' immigration.

Refugee Blues

Say this city has ten million souls,
Some are living in mansions, some are living in holes:
Yet there's no place for us, my dear, there's no place for us.

Once we had a country and we thought it fair,
Look in the atlas and you'll find it there:
We cannot go there now, my dear, we cannot go there now.

In the village churchyard there grows an old yew,
Every spring it blossoms anew:
Old passports can't do that, my dear, old passports can't do that.

The consul banged the table and said:
"If you've got no passport, you're officially dead."
But we are still alive, my dear, but we are still alive.

Went to a committee; they offered me a chair;
Asked me politely to return next year:
But where shall we go today, my dear, but where shall we go today?

Came to a public meeting; the speaker got up and said:
"If we let them in they will steal our daily bread";
He was talking of you and me, my dear, he was talking of you and me.

Thought I heard the thunder rumbling in the sky,
It was Hitler over Europe saying, "They must die";
We were in his mind, my dear, we were in his mind.

Saw a poodle in a jacket fastened with a pin,
Saw a door opened and a cat let in:
But they weren't German Jews, my dear, but they weren't German Jews.

Went down to the harbour and stood upon the quay,
Saw the fish swimming as if they were free:
Only ten feet away, my dear, only ten feet away.

Walked through a wood, saw the birds in the trees;
They had no politicians and sang at their ease:
They weren't the human race, my dear, they weren't the human race.

Dreamed I saw a building with a thousand floors,
A thousand windows and a thousand doors;
Not one of them was ours, my dear, not one of them was ours.

Stood on a great plain in the falling snow;
Ten thousand soldiers marched to and fro:
Looking for you and me, my dear, looking for you and me.

W.H. Auden, *March 1939*

From 'Ten Songs', *Collected Poems*

A Roof Over Our Heads

The Embankment

Once, in finesse of fiddles found I ecstasy,
In a flash of gold heels on the hard pavement.
Now I see
That warmth's the very stuff of poesy.
O God, make small
The old star-eaten blanket of the sky,
That I may fold it round me and in comfort lie.

T.E. Hulme

A Poem for Shelter

Who was so rich
He owned diamonds and snowflakes and fire,
The leaf and the forest,
Herring and whale and horizon -
Who had the key to the chamber beyond the stars
And the key of the grave -
Who was sower and seed and bread
Came of a black night
To a poor hovel with a star peeking through rafters
And slept among beasts
And put a sweet cold look on kings and shepherds.

But the children of time, their rooftrees should be strong.

George Mackay Brown

Helping to Keep Hope Alive

A Church in Stoke Newington, Hackney

On 2 May 1996 two bishops who sit in the House of Lords, the Bishops of Liverpool and Ripon, went to Rectory Road United Reformed Church in Stoke Newington on a fact-finding mission. They were accompanied by two other church leaders. These were the Reverend Janet Sowerbutts, Moderator of the Thames North Province of the United Reformed Church, and Bishop Victor Guazzelli, Auxiliary Bishop of the Catholic Diocese of Westminster.

A crucial debate on the Asylum and Immigration Bill was about to take place in the House of Lords. The bishops wanted to see for themselves what was happening to people seeking asylum who were no longer able to claim social security benefits.

The church leaders were able to meet a group of asylum-seekers at Rectory Road Church: eight people were staying there and the church would have liked to house more but lacked the facilities to do so.

The Reverend Lance Stone, minister of the church, appealed to more churches in the area to help with caring for asylum-seekers.

He said: "This is a clear and simple way for Christians to put their faith into practice."

Vigil on Day for the Disappeared, St Martin in the Fields, Trafalgar Square, London

VI. The Right of Appeal

We have already mentioned the fact that an asylum-seeker whose claim is refused has a right of appeal. This should ensure that even if the Home Office makes a wrong decision, **justice** will eventually be done. If a wrong decision is made by the adjudicators, then the person refused asylum may be in great danger. It has to be said that, as things stand at the moment, the chances of appellants winning their appeals are very small.

A successful outcome to an appeal against the refusal of asylum by the Home Office depends on a number of factors.

1. The appellant must have a good lawyer

If the asylum-seeker is represented by a good lawyer, he or she is much more likely to win. A good solicitor will go through the asylum claim very carefully with an asylum-seeker, helping the person to sort out any apparent contradictions. Often what appears to be a contradiction can be explained. A good lawyer will also make sure that all the relevant information is included. This will help to give an asylum-seeker the confidence to present his or her case adequately.

There are not enough solicitors and organisations able to take on the work of representing asylum-seekers. As a result, some asylum-seekers are not represented at all, and find themselves at a big disadvantage. In unrepresented cases the adjudicator should assist the appellant in order to see that justice is done, but this still does not compensate for good representation. There are also rogue solicitors who let their clients down.

The government has been asked to act against 'bogus' advice centres which mislead asylum-seekers and rogue solicitors and agencies. At the time of writing it has said it has no plans to do so.

2. The Home Office and the adjudicators must have a realistic assessment of a country's Human Rights record

Home Office officials are sometimes ignorant of the true situation in the country someone has fled from. Sometimes the Home Office assessment of a country is completely at odds with assessments by human rights organisations such as Amnesty International or Human Rights Watch. It has happened that, at the same time as the Foreign Office has been telling British citizens that they should not visit a country at all, the Home Office has been saying that it is safe to return failed asylum-seekers there.

3. The adjudicators must be able to assess credibility properly

It has already been pointed out that adjudicators may find it difficult to make a correct decision about a person's credibility. In spite of the efforts of the adjudicators to obtain good information, they still may not know enough about the culture of a country to know what is credible or not in an asylum claim. As a result they may be unable to decide correctly whether something is true or untrue. Medical evidence of torture is not always taken seriously.

4. The immigration regulations must be fair

The adjudicators must apply the relevant immigration rules. Many people think these are not entirely fair to asylum-seekers. As we have seen, it may count against asylum-seekers if they arrive with false documentation or no documentation at all; if they do not apply for asylum immediately upon arrival; or if the plane they came in made a stop-over in some other country.

5. The adjudicators must be independent minded

The adjudicators must be able to stand back and test the inconsistencies which the Home Office claims to have found in the asylum-seeker's testimony. The adjudicator must be able to take into account the trauma which the asylum-seeker may be suffering from, medical evidence of torture if that exists, and the asylum-seeker's hesitation and fear.

Other circumstances also militate against asylum-seekers

• Recent research suggests that some adjudicators are harsher than others, and that there are discrepancies between adjudicators about the human rights situation in some of the countries from which people flee. One adjudicator may decide that it is safe to return people to a particular country, whilst another may decide the opposite. This is a cause of great anxiety for both asylum-seekers and their legal representatives.

• Asylum-seekers who are refused asylum and who decide to appeal against the decision are no longer able to claim social security benefits. It is extremely difficult for destitute asylum-seekers to exercise their right of appeal. UNHCR says it is:

> "unable to see how a legal appeal right can be fairly accessed if the appellant is not given the assistance necessary to sustain him or herself in that period. The appeal right is rendered ineffective. This in turn undermines the ability of the United Kingdom to meet its regional and international treaty obligations."

• Asylum-seekers appealing against refusal of asylum are poorly protected. At an Industrial Tribunal hearing there is not only an adjudicator, but also two assessors to help see that a fair decision is reached. At an immigration hearing everything depends on just one adjudicator unless the appellant is allowed to take the case on to the full Tribunal on a point of law. Moreover, people who appear before an Industrial Tribunal will be able to use their own language and will suffer far less anxiety than asylum-seekers who go before an immigration adjudicator.

Pietermaritzburg, South Africa

Two Poems by Prisoners of Conscience

The beauty of this single tree
obedient to the season's icebound laws
and stoic under winter's knouts,
the fragile pathos of its tattered rags
still steadfastly unfurled
like unsurrendered flags
of some long-lost and gallant cause
a fecund and diurnal logic
conceived and brought about:
and this, this beauty of a single tree
redeems my lunatic
and stone and iron world.

By Dennis Brutus, imprisoned in South Africa on Robben Island.
From *Stubborn Hope* , Heinemann, 1978.

You took away all the oceans and all the room.
You gave me my shoe size in earth
   with bars around it.
Where did it get you? Nowhere.
You left me my lips, and they shape words
   even in silence.

By Osip Mandelstam, a Russian poet, who died in internal exile
after being imprisoned. From *Selected Poems*, Penguin, 1977.

Helping to Keep Hope Alive

UNHCR

The Office of the United Nations High Commissioner for Refugees

The UNHCR came into being in 1951 to provide protection for little more than a million refugees in Europe and North Africa. It had a mandate for just three years in the hope that solutions to the problem of refugees could be found in that short time.

Decade by decade since then its responsibilities have grown and its mandate has been extended, until by the mid 1980s over 15 million people were being helped by the UNHCR. It seeks to provide 'international protection' for refugees and it seeks 'permanent solutions' for their problems.

UNHCR has offices in over 120 countries worldwide as well as its Geneva Headquarters. In its work it makes use of other UN organisations: the Food and Agriculture Organisation and the World Food Programme, the World Health Organisation, UNESCO which helps give education to refugee children, the International Labour Organisation and the UN Development Programme (vocational training). Part of its remit is to repatriate people when circumstances change and they are able to return home.

It also co-operates with other international organisations such as the European Union and the Organisation of African Unity, as well as with thousands of voluntary organisations. These include the Refugee Council in the United Kingdom and the member organisations of its Overseas Committees such as Oxfam, CAFOD, Save the Children, Christian Aid, Jesuit Refugee Service, and many more.

UNHCR has a unique role to play in matters of co-ordination of aid, and in the protection of endangered people. To these ends it also seeks to inform and educate the public about the needs of refugees, and to urge the importance of dealing with the root causes of flight.

A Prayer for Detained Asylum-seekers

Lord Jesus,

You know how it feels to be a refugee;
to be rejected by your own flesh and blood;
to have no voice, no power, no home;
to be misunderstood, not heard.

In your love, Lord, have mercy on those
who turn to us for freedom, but find only a prison.

Have mercy also on us, for our failure to love,
and give us the grace and compassion
to care for those whose lives are in danger
and who seek asylum in our land.

Through Jesus Christ our Lord.

This prayer was written by a prison chaplain who has worked in a prison where asylum-seekers are detained.

Harmondsworth Immigration Detention Centre

VII. DETENTION

At the time of writing in mid-1996 about 700 asylum-seekers are detained in detention centres and prisons. About 10% of all asylum-seekers who arrive in Britain are detained for at least a short time. Some of them, perhaps after many months of imprisonment, will eventually be given full refugee status or exceptional leave to remain.

The UN High Commissioner for Refugees has repeatedly urged governments not to detain asylum-seekers because of the distress this causes. A recent survey by the UNHCR revealed that countries in Western Europe are increasingly resorting to detention of asylum-seekers. However, the UNHCR recognises that asylum-seekers will sometimes be detained, and says that, if so, they should not be detained in prisons together with 'common criminals'.

The Home Office says in a standard paragraph in letters on this subject:

> "It is Government policy to use detention only as a last resort. Temporary admission is granted wherever possible and detention is authorised only where there are good grounds for believing that the person will not comply with the terms of temporary admission. In deciding whether to detain, account is taken of all the relevant circumstances, including the means by which the person arrived in the country, any relevant immigration history, and any existing connections with the United Kingdom".

The refugee agencies and lawyers representing asylum-seekers are not satisfied by these asssurances.

Detention in Criminal Prisons: About a third of the detainees are held on the remand wings of criminal prisons. In some prisons they are mixed in with criminals in spite of the UNHCR Guidelines which say this should not happen.

> The kinds of people who are held on remand rather than given bail are those who are accused of very serious crimes including crimes of violence, people who already have a string of convictions, people who may be violent either to themselves or to others, and those who may interfere with witnesses.

Detained asylum-seekers are severely disadvantaged

They are held without being charged with or convicted of any offence. Under immigration law they may be detained for an unlimited length of time (some people have been held for more than 18 months). The Immigration Service does not have to give the detainee written reasons for detaining him or her. Most asylum-seekers have no recourse to the courts to get their detention reviewed. Habeas Corpus cannot be used. Only in a minority of cases do asylum-seekers have the right to ask for bail; the sureties required are usually several thousand pounds.

- **The European Council on Refugees and Exiles**, in a recent survey, shows that the United Kingdom detains more asylum-seekers than any other European Union country; it detains them for longer than any other European Union country; and the UK has fewer legal safeguards for detained asylum-seekers than any other European Union country.

- **Judge Stephen Tumin**, in 1989 when HM Chief Inspector of Prisons, reported on Haslar. This is a prison used as an immigration detention centre. He commented on:

> "the anxiety caused to these young men, who feel ... remote from friends and relations, inadequately advised, without recourse to legal aid, and, above all, in total uncertainty about the length of time for which they will remain in custody."

• **Boards of prison visitors** have repeatedly expressed concern that asylum-seekers are detained in criminal prisons and that the Home Office often fails to keep detainees informed about the progress of their cases.

• In 1994/5 **Amnesty International** published the result of a study they had carried out on fifty asylum-seekers who had been detained on arrival in the UK, and followed their cases through to a conclusion. Seven of these people were eventually granted full recognition as Convention refugees. Six people were detained for more than six months, three for more than 10 months. Twenty-two were held in criminal prisons for all or most of the time, including six of those eventually recognised as refugees. Those in criminal prisons found themselves detained with people charged with murder and other violent crimes, and with people who had a whole string of convictions behind them.

• **The Medical Foundation for the Care of Victims of Torture** studied forty-seven detainees whom their doctors had visited in prison or detention centres to make reports on allegations of torture. In 1994 they reviewed these cases in a report entitled *A Betrayal of Hope and Trust*. Most of the people they studied had been detained for between 3 and 8 months when seen by the Medical Foundation, one for more than 13 months, and another for 17 months. On two occasions the Medical Foundation was called in because asylum-seekers had tried to hang themselves.

• In 1994 the **UN Committee for the Prevention of Torture** visited Pentonville Prison where asylum-seekers were being held (they have since been moved to Rochester Prison). Among their recommendations was the following:

> **"steps to be taken without delay to bring an end to the practice of placing in prison establishments persons deprived of their liberty under the Immigration Act."**

The UK in its reply declined to do so.

But perhaps as a result of these and other pressures, in 1995 the Home Office began to concentrate most asylum-seekers in its designated Immigration Detention Centres and in just five criminal prisons, rather than scattering asylum-seekers throughout the prison service. They were moved away from some of the most unsuitable prisons. At Rochester Prison around 200 asylum-seekers are concentrated on special wings of the prison. Even so, there is still a scattering of detained asylum-seekers in a large number of prisons. The number of detained asylum-seekers has risen threefold since Judge Tumin made his comments in 1989.

Somewhere

Somewhere a mother sobs
through bomb-shattered nights
hunger drains the blood of children.
Somewhere we eat the sputum of our pride
when we know nothing and we blunder.
Somewhere a woman sees her sick man
teeter on the edge of midnight
and turn his back on her and all forever.
Somewhere in the arena we lose our head
amid the boos and jeers and whoops
along the sidelines.
Somewhere a mother awaits
her man, her son
in the chains of an oppressor
or waits for those who never come
and still endures we know not how.
And yet amid the smoking debris
of a fear-driven world
while man juggles with megaton eggs,
somewhere a woman gives the world
an artist:
a child who sings and dances,
dreams and weaves a poem
round the universe
plunging down the womb
to fire a cell
sinking down a borehole
to probe the spring of life
from where the earth will rise
to meet the sky.
Somewhere in ancient China, it is told,
a man made a song
out of the wailing of a dove
a song that moved all the animals
to rise and kill the serpent
who ate the bird's young ones.
To know our sorrow
is to know our joy -
Somewhere a mother will rejoice.

Es'kia Mphahlele, South Africa, *JRS Confidential*

Romas in Happy Hill, Banja Luka

VIII. FLIGHT: ITS 'ROOT CAUSES'

(Adapted from 'The Causes of Forced Displacement: The Breakdown of Sustainable Global Community' by Mark Raper, SJ; International Director, Jesuit Refugee Service).

The testimonies which refugees have contributed to this book help to give an insight into the reasons why people are sometimes driven to flee from their own countries and seek asylum abroad. This chapter tries to deal with this subject in a rather more systematic manner.

1. Individual and communal factors causing displacement

Why do people move?

To understand refugees and to understand why people are forced into becoming refugees, we must set this phenomenon in a broader context of migration and resettlement. As we have already seen, migrants include Western Europeans who move to other European countries or to America seeking to better themselves. Today, about 125 million people, including many UK citizens, live outside their countries of birth. Most leave home seeking:

- a better education for their children;
- better employment;

- life nearer other members of their family;
- a safer place in which to live.

What distinguishes a refugee from a migrant is the speed with which the decision to depart has to be made, as well as the coercion and fear which make the refugee decide to move. Refugees generally have little choice of destination, possibly being forced to flee to alien or inhospitable territory. Reasons for flight vary across a scale from alarming to urgent.

Consider the following reasons given for leaving home:

- To find schooling for my children; our schools were closed because of the war.
- To find a home for my family. Ours was destroyed in the fighting.
- To find work; my shop was burned, my fields were mined, my cattle were looted by the soldiers.
- To find a safe place near friends. Where I was living, anyone who looked like me or shared my beliefs risked arrest.
- To reach a safe place. Around us the violence never ceased.
- The hope of reunion with members of my family who are already refugees.

Not all of these reasons would qualify a person as a refugee under the terms of the UN Convention on Refugees.

The decision to flee or to take refuge may be sharpened by personal experiences such as:

- Fear of immediate attack, rape or violence, or the experience of these.
- Experience of detention without trial or political imprisonment.
- Experience of torture.
- Repeated attacks or death threats, especially where civic institutions fail to offer even minimal justice or security.
- Knowledge that all the members of one's political party, social group, religion or ethnic group are being targeted and persecuted.

Here we have reasons which suggest that the person who flees has 'a well-founded fear of persecution', and will qualify for refugee status.

We will not fully understand refugees unless we take account of their desire to return home. A desire to be able to return home is very strong among refugees.

Each Case Differs

Refugee case studies reveal that a mix of communal factors, as well as local and personal ones, lie behind most refugees' decisions to leave home.

- An amputee from Mozambique fled because of his physical plight which made it impossible for him to find work in his country's depressed economy.

- Someone from the Sudan had suffered repeated attacks with the threat of still more. This, coupled with massive internal displacement drove him to try to escape.

- For a young woman from Somalia and her family, rape was the final factor which galvanised them all to flee.

Violence on a broad front also has its effects at an intensely personal level. Conversely, rape and torture, while personal, are now used systematically to subdue populations. Systematic abuses create a thirst for revenge and sow the seeds of generations of destruction.

Many valid reasons for flight fail to fit within current legal definitions of a refugee. As we saw earlier, people who are persecuted by 'non-state agents' are unlikely to qualify for asylum although their governments are neither willing nor able to protect them.

> There also exist reasons for flight that elicit no one's sympathy and offer no valid reason for seeking protection. Those who commit violent crimes and then leave home for fear of reprisal, as in the case of some who have fled from Rwanda, deserve to be called to account.

External and Social Causes

• The multiple causes of forced displacement: war, civil conflict, human rights violations, colonial domination and persecution for political, religious, ethnic or social reasons characterise every region of the world, and are major causes of forced human displacement today.

• In many parts of the world there are severe breakdowns of economic and social conditions that once provided people with the means to survive in their traditional communities and in their own countries. This phenomenon is accelerating the movement of people.

• Environmental devastation has emerged as a powerful motivation for large-scale human displacement.

The Breakdown of Sustainable Community

• At one level, community is founded on the family. Again and again, today's conflicts target the family unit and bring about family breakdown. Earlier wars also broke the family apart: men left their wives behind at home to go and fight. Today, the men may be the ones left behind at home when the women and children flee, a switch of 'gender roles'.

• **Ethnic strife, factional strife and 'warlordism'** also break societies apart, and these, too, are found in many areas of the world. Bosnia and Rwanda are both good examples of this kind of breakdown.

• Between the need to flee and the decision to go, a potential refugee must weigh up **the feasibility of escape**. Some geographical factors make it easier: the proximity of international borders, the absence of major physical barriers, reasonable roads and facilities for travel. Ready access to airports leads to great numbers of asylum-seekers and migrants from every part of the world arriving, often 'irregularly', at any city with an international airport.

2. Other global developments which affect displaced-people

Warfare as Industry

Easily available light weapons are associated with rising levels of violence and social disintegration. Trade in small arms and the use of them goes with ethnic conflict and crime, and leads to increased displacement of people. Today's wars are becoming increasingly 'low-tech'. Low-tech landmines enjoy a booming trade.

The Weakening of the Nation-State

The nation-state, founded upon the once sacrosanct principle of sovereignty, has been weakened and even paralysed by recent global challenges. Huge international debts are often a cause of weakness in a state.

None of the causes of flight noted above exist on their own.

Yet the complex of interrelationships is difficult to unravel. By now, commentators can discern the main factors operating in Germany after World War I which created the soil in which Nazism could take root and grow.

- A faltering economy that left many unemployed.
- The existence of ethnic groups (in particular the Jews) available to be made into scapegoats.
- A demagogic leader who created and manipulated hatred, to gain power for his own purposes, and
- an economy ravaged by war and by huge reparations demanded by the victors of World War I, and dependent on arms production.

Today, we can see somewhat the same complex of factors in a number of refugee-producing countries.

We shall not be surprised to find that the church is not only concerned to assist people who are forced to seek asylum. It is also involved in a number of different ways in seeking to alleviate the conditions which result in people finding conditions intolerable.

- CAFOD, Christian Aid and Tear Fund are some of the church-supported groups working to alleviate poverty.

- Justice and Peace groups and the Catholic Institute for International Relations are concerned with human rights and viable and democratic political processes.

- The Religious Society of Friends (the Quakers) are actively involved in working for peace.

Nothing happened here.
There was no demonstration; there were never
young people singing in this square,
and if there were,

they went home in good order, filing out
at the army's direction. Or if not,
then you couldn't hardly wonder at what
you say they got,

though they didn't. Nobody died,
except soldiers in lightly defended
tanks, which were set upon, mob-handed,
by the misguided

counter-revolutionary anarchist
saboteurs (funded by the West
to ferment rebellion), who, as I stressed,
didn't exist.

Sheenagh Pugh

From *Selected Poems*, Seren Books, 1990

Why am I here? Help me, when I have been the victim of injustice, to find out why you have allowed it - what is the purpose of my suffering? Help me to have inner peace and freedom to look around and help those within the prison walls who could be ministered unto even by a fellow prisoner.

Yes, we know you are on the throne, but find it hard when we are victims of injustice. Let us know and be assured that you have got the whole world in your hands - that takes away the desire for vengeance.

Lord, there is blessing in suffering however hard it seems behind bars. To change the values of one's life, to be closer to you, to understand and serve others who suffer - teach us what you want us to learn. There are many things to learn.

O for faith, Lord, to move the mountains of fear and doubt. You have challenged us to challenge you - so give us the faith to overcome our fears and doubts.

From *The Prisoner's Lantern*: *Meditations by a Prisoner in Ethiopia*,
Keston College, 1988

This prayer was written by a Christian political prisoner in Ethiopia who was detained along with convicts.

Catholic Social Teaching and Migration

The Catholic Church bases her teaching about refugees and immigration on her more general basic principles for social life.

The key points are:

- The dignity of the human person
- The common good
- Responsibility of the powerful for the less powerful
- Solidarity
- The right to work
- Family unity

The Catholic Church takes a global, not a narrowly nationalistic, view of migration.

She puts a high priority on the generous and proper treatment of all migrants and refugees, no matter who they are, where they are, or how they have arrived.

This means that governments and the Church may look at questions about migrants, refugees and asylum-seekers from differing viewpoints.

Afro-Brazilian girls demanding their basic human rights on Good Friday in Sao Paulo, Brazil

IX. The Teaching of the Catholic Church

The Church's concern for refugees comes from her concern for the **dignity of the human person**. It is part of Christian belief that human beings are made in the image and likeness of God. And at the centre of our faith is God's revelation of himself to us in the man, Jesus.

Pope John Paul II in 'Refugees: A Challenge to Solidarity' has described the situation of refugees as "perhaps the greatest of all the human tragedies of our time". It is so because the sort of life a refugee is often forced to live tends to degrade the person physically, psychologically and spiritually.

Rights

The Church has developed a body of social teaching on the rights of migrants - both **emigrants** and **immigrants**. The landmark in the application of church teaching to social issues was Pope Leo XIII's encyclical letter *Rerum Novarum*. This described the connections between economics, migration and social justice. Even more importantly, Catholic social teaching includes a strong concern for the basic rights of involuntary migrants and refugees.

Pope John XXIII, too, was aware of the "sufferings - the incredible sufferings - to which they are constantly exposed". He makes it clear in *Pacem in Terris* that there is a "duty of state officials to accept" such refugees and - "so far as the good of their own community, rightly understood, permits - to further the aims of those who may wish to become members of a new society".

There is an important difference between migrants and refugees, and the humanitarian concerns of refugees leads the church to state their rights particularly strongly. "Any person in danger who appears at a frontier has a right to protection." Such acknowledgement by a host country "is not a simple concession made to the refugee: he is not an object of assistance, but rather a subject of rights and duties". But migrants have rights too, and the church believes that these also must be vigorously protected.

The main points of Catholic social teaching can be listed as follows.

1. **The dignity of the human person**: All human beings are created in the image of God and should be treated accordingly, no matter what their legal status is in society, and whether or not they are citizens.

2. **The common good**: Governments are responsible for creating conditions of justice in their societies and in the world. Governments have the right to control immigration in the name of the common good, but that right is not absolute. Because of the global common good, individual states have an obligation to provide protection and asylum for people who suffer persecution in their own countries. States also have an obligation to regulate immigration humanely.

3. **Solidarity**: Across borders and within societies, both individuals and governments have obligations to support less advantaged groups and people. The important Christian virtue of hospitality flows from an understanding of solidarity.

4. **The right to work**: One way in which people may participate in God's creative activity is through work. The Catholic Church believes that people who cannot support themselves and their families through work in their countries of origin, because of adverse conditions there, have a right to migrate in search of work. The Church insists on the right to movement in cases where a dignified working life is threatened by exploitation, economic poverty and discrimination.

5. **Family unity**: Families are the basic units of human society. The members of a family belong together, and keeping them together should be a guiding principle of social life. Keeping families together and bringing families together is just as important in the case of refugees and migrants as for the citizens of a country.

> **So we can see that the Catholic Church thinks in global, not narrowly nationalistic terms about migration. We can sum up the Church's teaching on this matter by saying that she puts a high moral priority on the generous and proper treatment of refugees and migrants, no matter who they are, or what their legal status is.**

The arrival of refugees and a state's decision to honour the international conventions governing their protection and status inevitably involve that state in having to make provision for the well-being of those who seek asylum within its borders. Host countries will have to establish procedures to deal with asylum applications, and this will inevitably be at public expense. Unaccompanied children, disabled people and other particularly vulnerable groups of refugees and asylum-seekers will require special provision if they are to be treated in a humane way.

But the individual refugees are not in themselves 'problems'. They are the victims of struggles for power in social, economic, and political life, forced from their homes by war, political and religious persecution and human rights abuse. Others are forced to move by famine and economic disaster, too often the result of conflict, war and the lust for wealth and power. Nor should they be seen simply as victims: they are survivors with the guts to try to make a new life.

The Church's message is that those who are lonely, abandoned, in exile or persecuted are not abandoned by God. In Christ, God shares the human experience of abandonment:

> "The Son of Man had nowhere to lay his head"; "He came unto his own, and his own received him not"; and on the Cross, Jesus cried, "My God, my God, why have you forsaken me?"
>
> (Luke 9:58; John 1:11; Mark 15:34)

The message of the Church, since its very beginning, is that Jesus was not abandoned by God for ever. In the end he was raised by God. The earliest Christian creed, found in I Corinthians 15:3-6, has this statement of faith, this message of **hope** at its centre.

How do refugees share this **hope**, this **resurrection experience?** It cannot simply be equated with going home when the regime from which they fled has changed, marvellous though that experience may be. It is a long-term hope. But Christian communities may be able to help refugees towards that hope by showing a loving hospitality.

Refugees are among the poor with whom the Church seeks to stand in solidarity. Pope John Paul II has stated in a document looking forward to the Third Millennium:

> "If we recall that Jesus came to 'preach the good news to the poor', how can we fail to lay greater emphasis on the Church's preferential option for the poor and the outcast? Indeed, it has to be said that a commitment to justice and peace in a world like ours, marked by so many conflicts and intolerable social and economic inequalities, is a necessary condition for the preparation and celebration of the Jubilee."

Roma father and son in Banja Luka, Bosnia

HELPING TO KEEP HOPE ALIVE

Jesuit Refugee Service

Jesuit Refugee Service (JRS) was set up, in 1980, in response to the overwhelming needs of Vietnamese and Cambodian refugees in Indo-China. The main way of working is by 'being alongside' refugees, whatever their ethnic group, religion, nationality, political belief or social group. JRS works wherever refugees find themselves, and offers whatever specialised services it can.

This 'being alongside' may involve actually living alongside the refugees, or it may mean being involved in helping them to plead their case for asylum to the authorities. The specialised services offered include direct relief work, pastoral work, counselling, providing legal services, being involved in education, and helping with development projects.

It quickly became clear that such services were needed in many different parts of the world. So JRS became active with refugees in and from Ethiopia and Eritrea, El Salvador, Guatemala, Sudan, Peru, Mozambique, Liberia, Rwanda, Burundi, Burma, to name but some of the places where they work. JRS is also active in the great European upheaval in the former Yugoslavia, and in Bosnia in particular.

The vision of JRS was summarised at a meeting of field workers in Kigali, Rwanda, in the summer of 1995:

"To join the Jesuit Refugee Service (JRS) is to embark on a journey of faith in the company of refugees. Normally we act in international teams with an aim to build up local partners. Our desire is to offer personal, flexible and effective service to those uprooted from their countries and families, especially the most vulnerable...

"We try to be loyal to a wide network of partners, around the world and locally, among them the refugees whom we accompany...

"JRS is ready to collaborate with all persons, communities and organisations which similarly seek the immediate and long-term good of refugees. Without in any way proselytising, we prefer to build up the resources of the local church that it might continue like-minded service. Founded by the Jesuit Order which continues to take responsibility for it, JRS is also charged with animating communities and institutions associated with the Jesuits that they might develop, whether in their own name or through JRS, direct and competent services to the forcibly displaced.

"JRS' style of service is human and spiritual, seeking the long-term good of the refugees, while not neglecting needs that are immediate and urgent. Our service is pastoral and educational, most often with a training component. The refugees are credible and poignant witnesses to the need for justice in the world today. JRS advocates actions for justice and for reconciliation of those who are estranged, so that our world might more fully reflect the greater glory of God..."

Together we can make changes

X. Action

There has been a procession of saintly people down the centuries, and in our own time, whose lives have demonstrated the love of God in solidarity with those persecuted or forced to leave their homelands.

The Jesuit **Peter Claver** cared for slaves cruelly transported from Africa to the Americas. In the last century **Charles Lwanga** in Uganda, together with many others, both Catholics and Protestants, suffered martyrdom in his resistance to the persecution of an abusive monarchy. Another nineteenth century century heroine was the Italian-born American, **Frances Xavier Cabrini**, who devoted herself to immigrants. Many of these encountered enormous difficulties in finding their place in the United States. **Maximilien Kolbe** and the Russian nun, **Mother Maria**, both gave their lives in order to save others in Nazi concentration camps in the Second World War during the genocide of Jewish people. **Bishop Paride Taban** stayed with his Southern Sudanese compatriots when they had no food, and moved with them when they had to move into exile. **Archbishop Oscar Romero** championed the uprooted and powerless in El Salvador, and was murdered by a death squad because of his courageous stance. In 1977 **Archbishop Janani Luwum** of Uganda was murdered when he led his people in resisting the violence of Idi Amin's murderous regime.

These stories of personal heroism in the face of persecution show that the societies in which these people lived were not completely rotten. There will always be groups of people who resist tyranny even though the majority may acquiesce in the abuse of power. The genocide in Rwanda in 1994 has been a very clear demonstration of a terrible evil lying at the root of one of the worst refugee crises of our generation. Yet, even during the dreadful slaughter, in which many Christians acquiesced, some people showed quite heroic selflessness. **Gorette Uwimana**, a housewife, took refuge at **St Famille Church** in Kigali during the genocide. She paid tribute to the Sisters who cared for her and her children:

> "The nuns were wonderful. I cannot imagine how many of us could have lived through the nightmare of life at St Famille without them. It is important that the world knows this."
>
> (*Rwanda, Death, Despair and Defiance*, Revised 1995 edition, page 926, African Rights).

There have also been terrible failures. The Church has, until very recently, discriminated against Jews and Muslims. For centuries Christians failed to realise that slavery robbed people of their human dignity, and was therefore contrary to the will of God. In one way or another, if we are honest, we all find ourselves guilty of prejudice from time to time.

Church teaching cannot be confined to the written word only. **Praxis** (i.e. *practice* or action: what we do, as distinct from what we say we believe) is as important as orthodox adherence to a creed. It is not enough to moralise about refugees, for instance; we must act justly towards them. The Catholic Church in England and Wales has frequently recommended that its members should adopt the basic approach developed by groups such as the Young Christian Workers Movement: **See>Judge>Act** (and then repeat the cycle). This can form the basis for all social analysis.

This book aims to help us to see and judge the way in which asylum is being dealt with in Europe, but it would be incomplete if it did not suggest ways of acting to address the issues.

1. Information

Read up (in the press, in journals and news reports) about the situation in some of the countries from where refugees are coming. You could also contact one of the following organisations to get further information about asylum-seekers, and find out how you might be able to help. A number of these organisations use volunteer helpers.

A Selection of organisations which help to *Keep Hope Alive*

Amnesty International, (British Section) 99-119 Rosebery Avenue, London EC1R 4RE (0171 814 6200).

Association of Visitors to Immigration Detainees, 53 Western Road, Winchester SO22 5AH (01962 863317). This organisation has regional branches throughout the country. Contact this address for the national co-ordinator.

CAFOD (Catholic Fund for Overseas Development) Campaign Section; find who your local group is through the Campaign Office, Romero Close, Stockwell Road, London SW9 9TY (0171 733 7900).

Churches Commission for Racial Justice, Inter-Church House, 35-41 Lower Marsh, London SE1 7RL (0171 620 4444).

Committee for Migrants, Catholic Bishops' Conference, 39 Eccleston Square, London SW1V 1PD (0171 834 0522).

Detention Advice Service, 244a Upper Street, London N1 1RU (0171 704 8007).

European Council on Refugees and Exiles, 3 Bondway, London SW8 1SJ (0171 582 9928).

Joint Council for the Welfare of Immigrants, 115 Old Street, London EC1V 9JR (0171 251 5675).

Justice and Peace Groups, contact the local diocesan office.

Jesuit Refugee Service, 162 Stockwell Road, London SW9 9TQ (0171 924 9424).

The Medical Foundation for the Care of Victims of Torture, 96 Grafton Road, Kentish Town, London NW5 3EJ (0171 813 7777).

Pax Christi, 8 Henry Road, London N4 2LH (0181 802 3223).

Praxis, Pott Street, London, E2 0EF (0171 729 7985).

The Refugee Council, 3 Bondway, London SW8 1SJ (0171 582 6922). (There are regional refugee councils in Birmingham, Manchester and Edinburgh).

Refugee Studies Programme and Documentation Centre, Queen Elizabeth House, 21 St Giles, Oxford, OX1 1LA (01865 270722).

Social and Pastoral Action (Diocese of Westminster), Vaughan House, 46 Francis Street, London SW1P 1QN (0171 798 9008).

2. Political Action

One simple form of political action is to state your concerns to your Member of Parliament. Some of the groups listed above may ask you to do so in relation to specific issues.

- Letters need to be fairly short (one side of A4 maximum).
- They should deal with just one issue.
- It is important to make sure of your facts before writing.
- Ask your MP to convey your question/opinion to the relevant Minister, and to let you know how the Minister responds. This should ensure that you eventually receive a letter sent to your MP and signed by the relevant Minister.
- Be courteous!

3. Prayer, fasting and sharing of goods

Political and social action do not take the place of other traditional forms of solidarity. These traditions have come down to us through the Church and have lost none of their importance. They are ways in which every person can express his or her solidarity with marginalised people.

4. Hospitality

At times of crisis, when other provisions fail, Church halls have been used as shelters for people newly arrived or for those with no homes. But usually hospitality is required on a more personal level; being aware of, meeting with, and talking to, newcomers in your parish or area. The personal encounter with just one asylum-seeker is often more educative than many discussions on asylum issues. The New Testament echoes the Hebrew Scriptures in the urge to give hospitality:

> **"Do not neglect to show hospitality to strangers, for by doing that some have entertained angels without knowing it."** (Hebrews 13:2)

Shall we meet again at home
To talk and sing again
To walk and sit again
In our homes?

Shall we meet at home?
What a meeting it shall be.
Shall we meet again
In the land of our love?
In the land of our dear hope?

Shall we meet again at home
And end the longing of home
And send the wrongling home
And from sorrow ever be free?

Anon

Return from exile

When the Lord restored the fortunes of Zion,
we were like those who dream

Then our mouth was filled with laughter,
and our tongue with shouts of joy;
Then it was said among the nations,
"The Lord has done great things for them."

The Lord has done great things for us,
and we rejoiced.

Restore our fortunes, O Lord,
like the watercourses in the Negeb.

May those who sow in tears
reap with shouts of joy.

Those who go out weeping, bearing seed for sowing,
shall come home with shouts of joy, carrying their sheaves.

Psalm 126

Further Reading

Amnesty International, *Asylum Seekers Detained in the United Kingdom*, Revised edition, 1994. Obtainable from Amnesty International, 99-119 Rosebery Avenue, London EC1R 4RE.

Bell, Adrian, *Only for Three Months, the Basque Children in Exile*, Mousehold Press, 1996.

Carey-Wood, Jenny et al., *The Settlement of Refugees in Britain,* Home Office Research Study No. 141, HMSO 1995.

Collinson, Sarah, *Beyond Borders: West European Migration Policy. Towards the 21st Century,* Royal Institute of International Affairs, 1993.

Exile, published bi-monthly, is the newsletter of The Refugee Council, 3 Bondway, London SW8 1SJ.

HM Chief Inspector of Prisons, *Report on HM Prison Haslar*, Home Office, 1989. This should be obtainable through the public library service.

Joly, Daniele, *Haven or Hell? Asylum Policies and Refugees in Europe*, Macmillan, 1996.

Journal of Refugee Studies, published three times a year by Oxford University Press, is an academic journal which should be available through the public library service. Enquiries to the Refugee Studies Programme, Queen Elizabeth House, 21 St Giles, Oxford OX1 3LA.

Liberty, *The Last Resort: violations of the human rights of refugees and asylum seekers*, Report 9, 1995. Obtainable from Liberty, 21 Tabard Street, London SE1 4LA.

Medical Foundation for the Care of Victims of Torture, *A Betrayal of Hope and Trust: Detention in the UK of Victims of Torture*, 1994. Obtainable from the Medical Foundation, 96-8 Grafton Road, London NW5 3EJ.

Refugees, published monthly, is the journal of the UNHCR, P.O. Box 2500, 1211 Geneva 2 Depot, Switzerland.

Pontifical Council for the Pastoral Care of Migrants and Itinerant People, *'Refugees: A Challenge to Solidarity'*, C.T.S., 1992.

Acknowledgements

We are grateful to the following for permission to reprint copyright material:

The Keston Institute, Oxford: prayers by an Ethiopian political prisoner, *The Prisoner's Lantern*, 1988.

Sheenagh Pugh and Seren Books: the poems 'Sometimes' and 'Nothing happened here...', *Selected Poems*, 1990.

Heinemann Publishers: 'The beauty of this single tree...' by Dennis Brutus, *Stubborn Hope, Selected Poems of South Africa and a Wider World*, 1978.

Faber and Faber Ltd: 'Say this city has ten million souls' ('Refugee Blues') from 'Ten Songs', by W. H. Auden, *Collected Poems*.

John Murray: 'A Poem for Shelter', by George Mackay Brown, *Selected Poems*, 1991.

Oxford University Press: 'You took away all the oceans...' by Osip Mandelstam, *Selected Poems*, Oxford University Press, 1973.

Biblical quotations are from the *New Revised Standard Version*.

Jesuit Refugee Service is unable to trace the author of the poem 'Mother who heard the child whimper...'. They would be grateful for any information so that they can make due acknowledgement.